The Ultimate Way

Golf Method

The Ultimate Way
Golf Method

IT'S A HIT!
The Secret To Effortless Golf

Chad Westra
Golf Teaching Professional

Dedication

First and foremost, I thank God for giving me the wisdom and understanding to teach the game of golf in a very unique way. I therefore, dedicate this book to the people that God has placed in my life.

To my Mom and Dad, Barb and Dwayne, for showing me what it means to work hard and be driven with a vision.

To my grandparents, Andy and Florence, who taught me many of the same principles through their 66 years of marriage and through building their own family business. It was through their business that I learned to do what you love, surrounded by those you love. My grandparents showed me how to keep the faith even through trials. I am grateful for my grandparents' drive, energy, and strength. They are no longer living and are deeply missed.

To Don, who was a local golf enthusiast and club maker. During middle school I was frustrated with golf until I met Don who restored the enthusiasm I needed for the game of golf. He showed a real love for life and taught me to be curious about golf. Don is no longer living and he too is dearly missed.

To my wife, Kirstin, who has been with me through dreams and visions. She has been a real helper. I thank you and appreciate your many skills. Much love.

To my kids—Tyler, Alex, and Abbie—you give me reason to work harder each and every day. I enjoy taking all of you to work, golfing, playing and eating together. I hope the time we spend together is just as meaningful as the time I spent with my family growing up. My dad and grandparents would be very proud of our family business and the time we have to spend together as a family.

To my golf students who have had tremendous results and positive comments throughout the years. Knowing that I have helped you has been very rewarding.

TABLE OF CONTENTS

Contents

Author's Preface

I have been around golf for over 30 years, with over 20 years and counting as a golf instructor. Like most everyone else, I grew up learning a complex golf swing. I took complicated golf lessons. Needless to say, golf was becoming very frustrating as I grew older. I was not having fun or success playing the game I grew up loving. I got to the point I almost quit. Thankfully I was very curious and never gave up.

I can remember an occasion on my home course of Moccasin Creek Country Club in Aberdeen, South Dakota. I was about 15 years old, standing on the 18th fairway, I took the club back about two feet and then stopped. I looked at the clubface asking out loud, *"What is this clubface supposed to do? Does it go straight back or does it turn?"* I believe in fate and know that only one Other heard me that day. Three years later, fate led me to attend the San Diego Golf Academy. While there, I met the Director of Instruction and my questions about the clubface started to be answered. That year a car accident kept me from golfing, which in turn allowed me to focus more on teaching. I began to develop my own teaching method, *The Ultimate Way.* Now over 20 years later, *The Ultimate Way* has been fine-tuned, thousands of students have been instructed and I now believe this is the time to share my teaching method with others.

The curiosity I had at the age of 15 in the middle of the fairway has grown a hundred fold since then. I am now the owner of a teaching facility and have a proven teaching method that has withstood the test of time for the past 20 years. I am grateful to share this wisdom with you, the learner. It is now time to teach *The Ultimate Way!*

Introduction

I will say it right away: you will not learn a golf swing method by reading this manual. Most, if not all, teaching methods emphasize a golf swing that focuses on frustrating swing mechanics and use complicated terminology. *The Ultimate Way-Golf Method* eliminates all that by teaching you how to simply hit the golf ball. The fact is, a golf swing should not be taught. But that is not how golf has been taught over the last hundred years. Tradition says, *"Learn a golf swing"*. Modern golf instruction uses fancy computers and complex terms that only make the instructor look smart and the student look frustrated. The well known instructor tries to impress you while at the same time frustrate you in the process. Here are just a few facts about any golf method that teaches a golf swing.

According to USGA, less than 1/10th of 1% of all male golfers will ever shoot a par round. The average male score is 97-100. The average handicap has stayed about the same for over 50 years. And from 20 years of my teaching experience, I can attest to all this and more. Golfers are still frustrated today, have no power or accuracy and think too much while they hit. Golfers have not improved. Technology today has only brought on frustration faster. The golf swing method has run its course no pun intended! It's time for a new way of learning. A new way that does not teach a golf swing. A new way that eliminates the thinking of complex golf terms. A method that is understandable and easy to learn. A method that teaches you how to hit and not over-think.

The Ultimate Way restores truth to the game of golf. The benefits are many. I hope you are ready to learn *The Ultimate Way*!

The Ultimate Way

Golf Method

Philosophy of *The Ultimate Way*

I said it before, *The Ultimate Way* is the only golf system that does not teach a golf swing. The truth is, a golf swing should never be taught; it's pointless. A waste of time. Unfortunately, that is what you will learn from most golf systems today. Not here. Get ready to learn a hit that produces a golf swing.

It's a Hit!

The Ultimate Way is innovative by showing that a hit creates a golf swing. *How?* Cause and effect. If you learn the hit you get a golf swing. I ask you this, *"what is easier to learn? One thing: the hit?, or ten things: a swing?"* **The answer, I hope, is·one thing; the hit.**

When you learn how to hit later in this book, you will learn the hit at different levels; building higher and higher until the hit looks like a golf swing. It is, however, a hit you're learning; not a swing.

The hit works because *The Ultimate Way* taps into hand-eye coordination; an automatic ability everyone possesses. Thoughts of the golf swing and the frustration that is created due to over-thinking are eliminated. There's just something about getting up to the ball and hitting it without detailed thinking. It really is a freeing feeling. A feeling a joy.

Golf could use a fresh start and a new way of learning. *The Ultimate Way* is the new way. With millions of frustrated golfers, a new way could restore hope to those who are so frustrated. Golf courses could be busier with more golfers who are now enjoying the sport. All this is possible with learning a new way-*The Ultimate Way*. Have fun reading and learning about the hit!

Foundation of *The Ultimate Way*

Before anything can become automatic, including the golf swing through hitting, there is a learning process everyone must go through. The learning process consists of three steps: cognitive, fine-tuning, and automatic.

In this book you will learn how to progress from the cognitive stage to the automatic stage of the learning process. You will also learn what happens in the learning process when the mind is cluttered with unnecessary swing thoughts.

Step One: COGNITIVE

The cognitive stage is the information stage. At first this stage creates awareness. How and what information is given will determine how much awareness one has; which will also determine a level of frustration.

If unnecessary information is given or communicated in an improper manner, awareness and frustration will be high and performance will be low. *The Ultimate Way* decreases awareness by teaching a hit that leads to an automatic golf swing. Progression to the fine-tuning stage of learning can now be achieved.

Step Two: FINE-TUNING

Learning a hit method, as taught by *The Ultimate Way,* taps into a fine-tuning ability that leads to an automatic golf swing. Traditional golf that uses a swing method, requires tapping into muscle memory and thus requires managing a series of complicated swing thoughts. The mind becomes overloaded and the swing becomes frustrating. When you are frustrated, you leave the fine-tuning stage of learning and go back to the cognitive stage of learning, where awareness and frustration is especially high. Not surprisingly, performance is also low.

Learning to hit *The Ultimate Way* taps into fine-tuning which leads the student toward the automatic stage of the learning process.

Step Three: AUTOMATIC

The automatic stage of the learning process is when a task is free of unnecessary, detailed thinking. Let's look at this closer by considering other sports for a moment. A quarterback does not think about his shoulders when he throws a football nor does a baseball player think about his hips when he hits a baseball. Likewise, a basketball player does not think about his or her arms when shooting the basketball. *So why would you think about your shoulders, hips, or arms when hitting a golf ball?*

Any teaching method that focuses on a complicated golf swing will take a student back to the *cognitive stage* of the learning process, where frustration is high and learning toward the automatic stage is hindered or stopped.

The Ultimate Way is the only golf method which promotes automatic learning by fine-tuning the hit.

Proper Communication

Not only is there a learning process which aids the hit in becoming automatic, but also a dominant learning style in which people communicate that promotes optimal learning. A student's preferred communication style may be either visual, auditory, or kinesthetic. A visual learner prefers to see things, an auditory learner prefers to hear things, and a kinesthetic learner prefers to feel things. Approximately 60% of all golfers are visual, 20% are auditory, and 20% are kinesthetic learners.

As a golf instructor, it is very important to determine a student's **dominant** communication style and adapt teaching to how a student prefers to communicate. A golf student cannot learn optimally if they cannot communicate effectively with their golf instructor. When miscommunication occurs, the student will have difficulty making sense of the information the instructor has given them. Therefore, students learn best when their dominant communication style is used to **maximize effective communication, and in turn minimize awareness and frustration.**

<u>VISUAL LEARNER</u>

A visual learner is the most common style of learning. Individuals who have a dominant visual learning style like to **see** things demonstrated.

As an instructor, I will stop the club at various positions, so the student can **see** what the clubface looks like. I can often sense when a person is visual, because they like to keep to their space. They often shake hands to greet people and then back up. As a result, it is important that as a golf instructor I do not crowd a visual learner or invade their space. With this type of learner, I tend to keep my distance after giving instruction; sometimes backing up 10 to 20 feet.

Most younger students are visual. They often learn by mimicking those they golf with. Whether good or bad, I once had a student who golfed right-handed and his young child mimicked him by golfing left-handed. Eventually some young golfers will develop a different dominant learning style as they get older.

   If you have determined that you are a visual learner, you will benefit from the drawings in this book. You may also learn best by watching DVDs of *The Ultimate Way*.

AUDITORY LEARNER

   A person who is an auditory learner communicates best through *verbal* swing cues as to capture rhythm they are seeking.

   During instruction, key words or numbers can be used to trigger rhythm. The mistake many rhythmic players make is to seek rhythm through body motion. Motion is the number one cause of being inconsistent. This is why, I instruct auditory learners to count during the hit. Counting gives them the rhythm they are seeking, which in turn allows them to stay still.

   How to count: Certain positions are assigned a number. For instance, the takeaway is triggered by counting the #1, with the upswing triggered by counting the *#2,* and finally the impact, or the hit, is triggered by counting the *#3* aggressively. How fast or slow these numbers are said determines the rhythm or tempo. The #1 and #2 are slower than the hit or #3. Save your energy for the hit.

   If an auditory student needs to work on a particular area of their swing, I will refer to the number they are counting such as, "*go to #1*". For an auditory learner this triggers a visual picture, in this case, the takeaway. Proper communication allows the auditory student to learn properly. Without rhythm, an auditory learner will be frustrated.

   Communicating the golf swing to an auditory learner in any other manner, will only result in high awareness and frustration.

KINESTHETIC LEARNER

A kinesthetic learner understands the golf swing by breaking it down into *positions*; relating each position to a ***feeling.***

The takeaway is referred to as *position (1),* the upswing as *position (2),* the downswing as *position (3),* and the hit as *position (4).*

A kinesthetic learner should practice each position again and again to acquire the feel, before proceeding to the next position. The golf swing will look something like a dot-to-dot. Once the feel has been captured, the golf swing smooths out. It is important for a kinesthetic learner to keep practicing this way, because feelings wear off and do not last. Even if a student practiced yesterday, the feel is gone and he or she will have to regain the feel by practicing each position again.

Only by practicing positions over and over, will a student get the feel back. So hitting lots of balls is really not necessary with a kinesthetic learner. In fact, when I teach this student, it is not uncommon for most of the range balls to remain in the bucket after a lesson. A student might practice position (1), the take-away, five times before they actually hit a ball.

Practicing any other way would hinder a kinesthetic learner's progression towards a feeling, and they would see little progress in attaining an automatic golf swing.

Communication Style

Identifying a student's dominant communication style is key to *The Ultimate Way* teaching method. Today, most traditional golf lessons do not focus much on how a student learns. Instead, the golf student is required to adapt to their golf instructor. Unfortunately, this is a mistake, and a reason why so many students get frustrated when they take golf lessons. As a golf instructor, it is my job to change how I communicate, not the student's job to change to the instructor's preferred communication style.

Before the first lesson, I will have the student fill out a student survey. One question I ask is, *If you are learning a new task, which do you desire more: to see it?, hear it? or feel it? (circle one)*. Sometimes the student is not sure how they learn best. They may mark an answer with uncertainty, so I will also rely on personal observations to best identify their dominant learning style.

For instance, a student's vocabulary is a give-away in helping me determine their dominant learning style. They may say, *the grip feels good*, or *when I slice, it feels like...* This student is most likely a kinesthetic learner. Or they may say, *I just cannot get rhythm when I hit; my timing is off.* This student is probably an auditory learner. Another student may say, *how does my takeaway look?*, or *show me how it is done*. This student is likely a visual learner.

The clues are there! Without proper communication, it does not matter how great the golf method, the student will not learn properly and will undoubtedly become frustrated.

As we proceed in learning *The Ultimate Way,* I will assume that you know your dominant communication style. Detailed drawings for visual learners, and detailed explanations for auditory or kinesthetic learners, will be included throughout this book to further assist you in learning. Let's continue next to the fundamentals.

Fundamentals—The Foundation

When describing the grip, left- or right-hand descriptions will not be used. Instead, I will refer to the top hand as the hand closest to the end of the club, and the bottom hand as closest to the clubhead. By simply changing the words, it is easier to communicate with left hand golfers.

The grip is very important to achieving greater accuracy and distance. For this to happen, the hands must work together as a unit. If anything can ruin a grip, it is tension. In other words, squeezing the club too tightly. The right grip can help.

There are three grips to choose from: interlock, baseball, and overlap grip. First, I believe the interlock grip actually causes tension especially when the pinkie interlocks with the forefinger. The baseball grip is acceptable for younger golfers, or beginners but as they get older or start to improve, a switch to the overlap grip is recommended.

The best grip for decreasing tension is the overlap. Making the overlap grip the preferred grip of *The Ultimate Way*. It allows you to hold onto the club as if you had a baby bird in your hand.

The Top Hand—Step 1

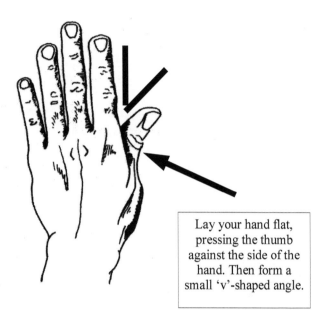

Lay your hand flat, pressing the thumb against the side of the hand. Then form a small 'v'-shaped angle.

By forming a 'v'-shape at the tip of the thumb, you get a more consistent grip. Likewise, when the thumb is apart, not forming a 'v', the grip is more inconsistent.

The Top Hand—Step 2

Lay the grip diagonally across the fingers.

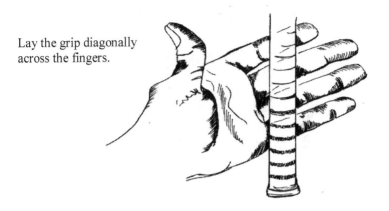

The Top Hand—Step 3

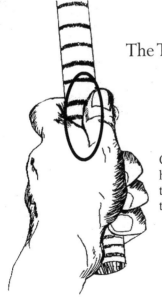

Close the fingers and rotate the hand onto the club; keeping the thumb pressed against the side of the hand.

The Bottom Hand

Lay the bottom hand flat. Form a small 'v'-shaped angle with the thumb pressed against the side of the hand. Once the 'v' is formed, lay the grip across the middle of the fingers. To decrease tension, keep the grip away from the palm where tension is created.

Step 1

Form a "v" shape with the thumb and lay the club across the middle of the fingers.

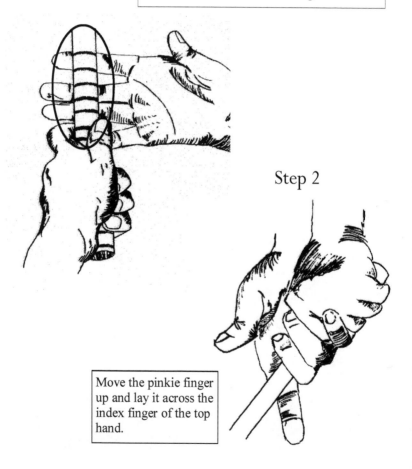

Step 2

Move the pinkie finger up and lay it across the index finger of the top hand.

The Bottom Hand

Close the fingers and drop the bottom hand onto the club, covering the thumb of the top hand.

Final Step

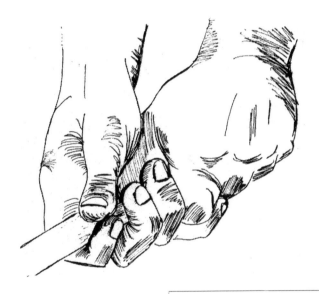

To avoid tension, the thumb of the bottom hand will also be pointed off to the side of the shaft. It may touch the index finger.

Ball Position

Now that the grip is getting more comfortable, add ball position. Short irons require the ball to be played in the middle of the stance. This includes all wedges - 6 iron. For longer clubs, the ball must be played off the front heel. This includes all woods, hybrids and 1-4 irons. The five iron is a club that may be played in either position; whichever feels more comfortable. Achieving proper ball position requires an alignment routine. Walking up to the ball and guessing does not work very well. However, first you should understand why the short irons must be played in the middle of the stance and the longer clubs off the front heel. Understanding this requires an explanation of the term "swing-center".

"Swing-center"

Swing-center

The swing-center determines where the low point of the club will be at impact. To locate the swing-center, take a golf club with one hand and hold it out in front of your body. Start it in a pendulum motion with the other hand. The club will move in an arch just like the golf swing. The low point of the club will be located in the middle of the body. This low point is controlled by the center of your head or swing-center. If the swing-center or head moves, so does the low point of the club. Moving the head during the swing, increases the chances of hitting the ball fat or thin.

Due to the swing-center, the shorter clubs require the ball to be played in the middle of the stance. If the swing-center stays still and your hitting technique is correct, the ball will be struck with a descending blow and a divot will be taken after impact.

Shorter Irons

When using the longer clubs, it is important that the ball be played off or near the front heel. This will allow the ball to be struck as the club is coming up; resulting in no divot.

If the swing-center stays still and your hitting technique is correct, you will automatically hit down with the irons and up with the woods.

Longer Clubs

Aiming Incorrectly

A golfer who aims incorrectly walks up to the ball, and starts dancing the feet until they think the body is lined up to the target. When in fact, the body should be parallel to the target, with only the clubface aimed at the target. The diagram below shows the body parallel to the target. To assist in aiming the body correctly, I have created a ball position routine that will help in lining up both the clubface and the body correctly.

Wrong Alignment

Body Parallel

Ball Position Routine

To achieve proper ball position, the clubface must first be lined up to the target. Align the clubface by standing behind the ball. Draw a line from your target to the ball. Pick a spot about 6 inches in front of the ball. This spot is now the target and it's this spot that you square the clubface up to when you walk up to the ball (*see the diagram below*). It's much easier to square up to a spot in front of the ball, rather than a flag 200 yards away. Now that the clubface is lined up, proceed by aligning the body parallel to the target.

Body Alignment

Now position your feet together; allowing the leading edge of the club to run directly between your feet. You should now have a 90 degree angle from your feet to the line coming off the ball to the target. The line coming off the clubface represents the body.

Target line: clubface is
square to this line.

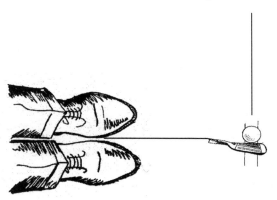

Body line: makes a
90 degree angle
through your feet.

Proper Distance from the Ball

Before separating the feet, pay attention to proper distance away from the ball. There should be about a fist-length distance from the end of the club to the body, or 4 to 6 inches. Adjust if you need to by moving closer or further away.

4 to 6 inches
away from
your body
and the end
of the club

Do not separate your feet until
you are proper distance away
from the ball.

Shorter Clubs:
#5, 6, 7, 8 & 9 Irons & Wedges

Once you have a 90 degree angle, separate your feet in this order:

Step 1

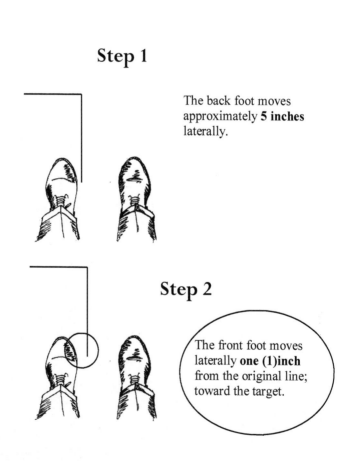

The back foot moves approximately **5 inches** laterally.

Step 2

The front foot moves laterally **one (1)inch** from the original line; toward the target.

After moving the front foot 1 inch, turn the toes of the front foot out approximately 20 degrees (*see the diagram below*). If the front foot was to remain straight, you would feel some pain in the hip area after releasing the club. Turning the front foot out assures comfort, and allows the body to rotate and finish balanced over the front foot after impact. After turning the front foot out, the ball is now positioned properly in the middle of the stance. If the stance is too narrow or wide, the back foot may be adjusted laterally. The front foot should **never** be adjusted.

The front foot turns out to allow for a weight shift.

Step 3

Longer Clubs:
#2, 3 & 4 Irons
#1, 3, 5, 7 & 9 Woods

Start with the same routine as for the shorter clubs. Position both feet together and move the back foot about 5 to 7 inches laterally. The difference is that the front foot does not move laterally one inch; it simply **turns**. If this feels too wide or narrow, again, the back foot may be adjusted. I often move my foot wider. Remember, the front foot should never be adjusted. Following this routine will allow you to consistently position the ball off the front heel every time. No more guessing!

Step 1

Move the back foot laterally about 5 inches to start the routine.

Turn the front foot slightly. The ball is now played off the front heel.

Step 2

Proper Posture

A good posture assures that the body is **balanced** during the swing; allowing you to hit more solid shots. To achieve a proper posture, the weight should be placed on the balls of the feet in the address position.

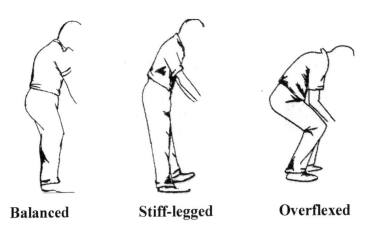

Balanced   **Stiff-legged**   **Overflexed**

Poor Posture

When weight is not balanced, poor posture is created; which causes you to fall forward or backward at impact. As a result, the ball is hit off the hosel or toe; resulting in lost distance.

Poor posture often occurs because golfers are told to bend their knees and sit down like on a bar stool—big mistake. Don't bend your knees like you are going to sit down at the bar. Come on, you are golfing, not buying a drink.

If you bend the knees too much, the body will purposely seek out a balanced or athletic position during the swing. Therefore, during the swing, the body will actually stand-up, causing a top or thin shot to occur.

If you stand up at the beginning and stay in an athletic position, the body will not adjust during the swing. The key is to stay balanced. Do not become stiff-legged by standing up too much or become overflexed by sitting down too much.

The Shank

This shot seems to frighten many people, but do not worry. A shank can be corrected by adjusting posture.

If the knees were overflexed, the weight would be positioned on the **heels** in the address position. Starting with too much weight on the heels causes the body to seek out a balanced position during the swing. At impact the weight is transferred from the heels to the toes. The hosel is moved closer to the ball, and a shank is the result.

A proper posture; with your back-end pointing up in the air, allows the weight to be positioned correctly on the middle of the feet. The body stays balanced and a shank is fixed!

Toeing

Hitting the ball off the end of the clubhead is called toeing the ball; which is the opposite of a shank.

This happens when too much weight is positioned on the toes at the start of the swing. The body will again seek out a balanced position during the swing; causing you to end up on your heels at impact. This forces the club to slide closer to the body and results in a shot hit off the toe.

Eliminate Frustrations

Hand-eye coordination is an untapped, automatic ability
that everyone possesses. It involves the use of fine motor
skills. *The Ultimate Way* teaches the golfer how to hit by tapping into this ability. Unfortunately, golf has been and contin-
ues to be mainly learned by using gross motor skills. For example: turn your shoulders, swing plane, hip rotation, left arm
straight, and just about anything else that focuses on the body.
The result is a very complicated golf swing. This teaching
method requires muscle memory and is designed for golfers to
think, think, think. Ultimately this leads to frustration and is the
#1 reason golfers take lessons. *The Ultimate Way* is the only
golf method designed to tap into your automatic ability to use
fine motor skills. Let's discuss fine motor and gross motor skills
further.

Fine-Motor Control
   Fine-motor control is the coordination of neurological func-
tions that coordinate muscles in the shoulder, elbow and hands.
Fine-motor control requires small, precise movements; like that
required when using a tool. Think of the golf club as your tool.

Gross-Motor Control
   On the other hand, gross-motor skills involve controlling
larger muscles in the body. Take for example, waving an arm.

The Brain 101
   To demonstrate just how important fine-motor skills are to
hitting a golf ball, I must first discuss my least favorite subject,
"the brain".
   There are five basic parts of the brain. The brainstem, mid-
brain, cerebellum, limbic system, and cortex or the "executive

branch". As information is taken in by sight or the other senses, the information is sent to the brain through neurons. Neurons are what cause the muscles to move. The cerebellum is a neural pathway which coordinates movement and balance with the motor cortex. Axons from the primary motor cortex descend to the spinal cord via two groups to make the muscles move. A lateral group receives 80% of the neurons to support fine-motor movement of the hand/finger, face, neck, tongue, eye, fore and hind limb muscles. A ventromedial group receives 20% of neurons, which control gross-motor skills such as posture, trunk movements, muscle tone, and upper leg and trunk muscles*.

These facts are conclusive; fine-motor skills have more brain power (80%) than gross-motor skills (20%)*. In fact, the precise hand movements are just what is needed to hit the golf ball. The hands hold onto the golf club just like a tool. For example, to effectively use a hammer or screwdriver, fine-motor skills are required to make the tool work properly.

Let me sum it up for you. Gross-motor skills would be used to wave your arms, walk, or lift something up. So use gross-motor skills when walking to your golf ball or waving to the crowd, but use fine-motor skills when hitting the ball. Best of all, tasks that tap into fine-motor skills and use hand-eye coordination, will be free of detailed thinking and frustration.

I encourage you to learn how to play golf by tapping into your fine-motor skills. Learn how to use the golf club as a tool, in a specific manner to hit the ball. Rather than tapping into gross-motor skills in an effort to learn a complicated golf swing. The traditional way of teaching students to use gross-motor skills has proven ineffective. According to USGA, less than 1/10th of 1% of all male golfers will ever shoot a par round. The average male score is 97-100. The average handicap has stayed about the same for over 50 years.

*80% to 20% http://wings.buffalo.edu/aru/Chpt08.ppt#293,14,Corticospinal Tract

Gross Motor Skills and Thinking

Are you ready for all the detailed thinking that gross motor skills require, like shoulder turn, hip turn and more (see diagram below)? All this thinking does one thing; creates awareness and that leads to frustration. Gross motor skills are just that; **gross**.

Thinking, Thinking, Thinking = Frustration!

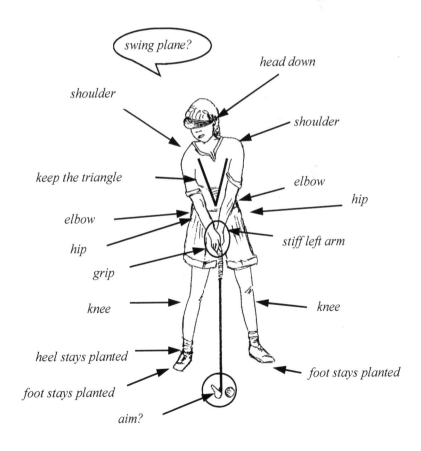

Over-Thinking

I call this "gross motor skill overload". This is the main reason golfers come to see me. Not because of a slice or hook, just sheer frustration or over-thinking.

If you are trying to learn based on muscle memory, let me share something you may already know. You must hit a lot of range balls. You have to hit, hit and hit. Basically, quit your day job and practice like a pro. Gary Player, a Hall of Fame Golf Pro, had time and drive to hit over a million golf balls in his career.

Do you have that kind of time? Probably not; few golfers do. This is what happens when you try to learn by using gross motor skills or muscle memory.

The Ultimate Way eliminates learning a swing; less thinking, less frustration and no need to hit a million golf balls. Keep your day job. Simply fine-tune the hit and see your game improve without all that detailed thinking.

Do you have time to hit over a million golf balls?

The Clubhead Advantages

Before learning how to hit, let's discuss the advantages to hitting properly; clubhead speed, effortless power, and accuracy.

Clubhead Speed

Clubhead speed can be gained by learning how to hit and use the clubface correctly. Clubhead speed is measured by figuring the rotation of the end of the clubhead. The goal is for the toe of the clubhead to be traveling **faster** than the heel at impact, which in turn, produces positive clubhead speed and effortless power. When the toe of the club is open or traveling *slower* than the heel, negative clubhead speed results, and a slice is produced. *Sound familiar?*

The box represents clubhead speed.

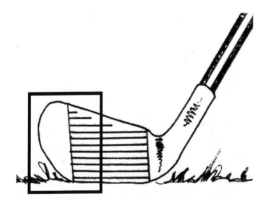

Shaft Speed

Everyone has shaft speed. It can only be generated in a positive manner. Shaft speed is **seen,** based on a player's tempo, whereas clubhead speed is *not seen.* Some players like John Daly swing very fast. Fred Couples, on the other hand, swings very easy. *What happens when you combine shaft speed with negative or positive clubhead speed?* Herein lies the secret to effortless power.

The box represents shaft speed.

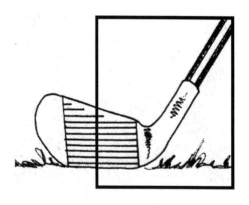

The "Pro" vs. The "Amateur"

Let's compare two players. A pro, who uses the clubface correctly and creates effortless power and accuracy, and the amateur, who uses the clubface incorrectly and creates loss of power and no accuracy. To make our comparison even more interesting, both players will have identical shaft speeds of 100 mph.

So what is the key difference in the two players?

It's how each one uses the clubface when they hit. The pro uses the clubface correctly by rotating it at impact. Thus, generating positive clubhead speed with tremendous accuracy. Fred Couples, when describing the proper technique to teaching the swing, says that it should be *"a natural, free-flowing, balanced, speed-producing, swinging action of the <u>clubhead</u>"**.

On the other hand, the amateur tries to hit with a square club-face at impact and actually opens the clubface which causes a slice. Thus, negative clubhead speed is produced, causing lost distance and accuracy.

The golf swing should be
"a natural, free-flowing, balanced, speed-producing, swinging action of the clubhead".
Fred Couples

The Pro: Positive Clubhead Speed + Shaft Speed

The pro rotates the clubface at impact; generating positive clubhead speed. Let's say the rotation of the clubface at impact produces a positive clubhead speed of 20 mph. Added to a shaft speed of 100 mph, a total speed of 120 mph is produced. But since clubhead speed is hidden, you can only see 100 mph which makes the pro's hit look effortless.

The Pro

100mph—Shaft speed (can be seen)
 20mph— Positive clubhead speed (not seen)

120mph—Total speed
100mph—What you see!

Positive Clubhead Speed = Toe Rotating

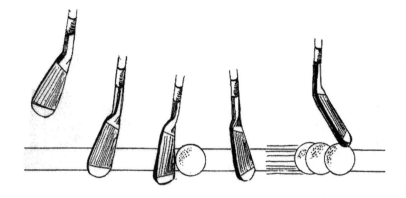

The Amateur: Negative Clubhead Speed + Shaft Speed

The amateur, trying to hit with a square clubface, actually opens the clubface at impact which causes a slice. Let's say a negative clubhead speed of 20 mph is produced. Subtracted from a shaft speed of 100 mph, the amateur has a total effective speed of 80 mph. However, you still see 100 mph because club-head speed is hidden.

The Amateur

100mph—Shaft speed (can be seen)
20mph—Negative clubhead speed (not seen)

80mph —Total speed
100mph —What you see!

Negative Clubhead Speed = Toe Opening

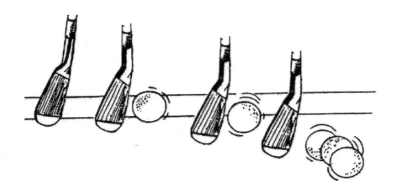

The amateur looks like the pro when swinging based on temp. But that is where the similarities end. The pro generates a hidden power that makes the hit effortless. While the amateur, swinging with the same speed, uses the clubface in the opposite manner and as a result has no power or accuracy.

Accuracy

Besides effortless power, accuracy is gained when the clubface is used correctly. Accuracy is simply an advantage, which means that you get accuracy.

Who do you think has an accuracy advantage? Someone who knows how to use the clubface, or someone who does not know how to use the clubface? Of course, only when you understand how to use the clubface properly, *The Ultimate Way,* will give you greater accuracy.

Now let's learn the technique in using the clubface to hit effortlessly and more accurately than ever before.

N ow that you know the advantages in using the clubface correctly (effortless power and accuracy), let's learn the technique in hitting *The Ultimate Way*. It starts by learning (4) Basic Positions:

#1 The Takeaway
#2 The Upswing
#3 The Downswing
#4 The Hit

The Order of Learning

The (4) basic steps are taught over a series of 1 to 3 lessons. You might think that these steps are taught in order, 1- 4, but they are not.

I start by teaching my students # 1 *The Takeaway* and then #4 *The Hit* . To aid in learning #1 & #4 together, I have created what I call *the clubface drill.* The clubface drill is the hit, in its shortest form. This is golf. The very reason you take golf lessons. You want to learn how to hit. This doesn't mean that it must be a complicated golf swing.

Now, let's look more closely at the steps to the hit.

It's a Hit!

The Takeaway

The Ultimate Way uses a wrist takeaway. Practice by using an eight or seven iron. Place the ball in the middle of your stance. Begin the takeaway with a turning of the wrist of the top hand. Watch the clubface, it actually turns in the first 12 inches just ever slightly. Then proceed bending the wrist up so the shaft is parallel to the ground and the clubface is toe-up. For more details see the first picture on the front cover. The takeaway or Step 1 is now complete. You are on your way to an effortless hit.

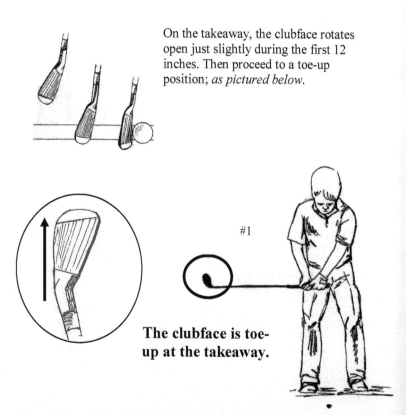

On the takeaway, the clubface rotates open just slightly during the first 12 inches. Then proceed to a toe-up position; *as pictured below.*

#1

The clubface is toe-up at the takeaway.

Focus When Cupping

Exactly what should you focus on when cupping the wrist of the top hand? Well, to be specific, I focus on the spot pictured below. You can actually see this spot and feel it bend when you cup your hand. Find the spot by putting your finger on it and bend your hand. Now, on the takeaway, upswing, downswing, & even during the release, focus on this spot. By focusing on this spot, hand-eye coordination will always be active. Many golfers focus on their arms and shoulders. As a result, their focus is on gross-motor skills, rather than on fine-motor skills used in hand-eye coordination.

The Key is to Focus on: 1,2,3&4

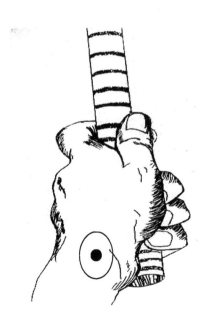

The Wrist Takeaway

The Ultimate Way takeaway is not a traditional arm or shoulder takeaway. It's a wrist takeaway. With this takeaway you will control the clubface better, trigger hand-eye coordination, and gain a more consistent takeaway. A wrist takeaway allows you to avoid all the frustration and inconsistencies that a traditional takeaway causes. With a traditional takeaway you do not trigger an automatic ability, but rather, you trigger gross motor skills that create frustration.

The Ultimate Way wrist takeaway helps to keep your body still, taps into your fine-tuning, and allows the takeaway to become automatic. The takeaway comes down to this: if the beginning is wrong, the rest is wrong. The wrist takeaway is a consistent takeaway; one that can easily be repeated.

Critics say:

Do not use your wrists! Tell that to a basketball player shooting a jump shot. Tell that to a quarterback throwing a football or wide-receiver catching a football. Tell that to a pitcher throwing a pitch, a batter hitting or an infielder catching a grounder and then throwing the runner out. Tell that to a bowler, dart thrower, pool player, or volleyball player. Golf is no different.

Daily activities such as typing, opening a door, or starting your car require the use of wrists too. The idea that wrists are not important to accomplish a task is utterly absurd. Your wrists tap into your hand-eye coordination, allowing you to fine-tune so the task can become automatic. Your wrists are key.

Auditory learners desire rhythm. This is achieved by counting #1 on the takeaway. A number also triggers a visual picture of the takeaway. A teacher can simply say *"go to #1"*. The student now understands.

Kinesthetic learners desire a feel. This is achieved by breaking the golfswing into positions. For example, the takeaway is referred to as *position (1)*. Repeatedly practicing the positions will capture a desired feel.

When you complete the takeaway, the shaft should be parallel to the feet; not inside or outside of the target line. The clubface should be toe-up or slightly open. Again, use only the wrist of the top hand on the takeaway.

The club is parallel to the target line.

Releasing the Clubface

Once you have completed a successful takeaway or #1, you

4 are ready to learn the hit, or release of the clubface. The release is from waist height of #1 to waist height of the follow-through. The release is the hit. It is why you play golf. At #1, rotate both hands to a finish at waist height. The clubface will be toe-up and the shaft will be parallel to the feet. See the second picture on the front cover for more details.

The Release

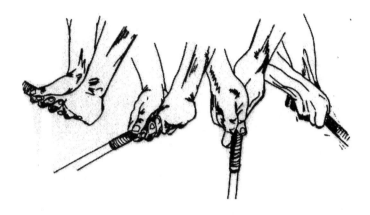

A Tour Pro—Release

A tour pro rotates the clubface 30 degrees (12) inches before and after the ball. They do not hit the ball with a square club-face.

As Fred Couples says,
"Let the clubhead fly."

15 degrees open

15 degrees closed

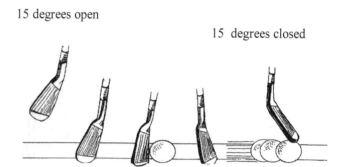

At impact the clubface
is 1.5 degrees open.

The average PGA Tour Pro has the clubface 15 degrees open (6) inches before impact (measured from the center of the ball) with a rotation of 2.5 degrees per linear inch. At impact the clubface is still 1.5 degrees open; not square. Then (6) inches past the ball the clubface is 15 degrees closed; not square.

AJ Bonar, Teaching Pro

41

The Release—A New Mindset

The release is a technique, but you must first have a new mindset in order to change technique. A traditional release is all about swinging at the ball, by releasing the body and then thinking about it. This is an old mindset. This is a source of much frustration for many golfers. It's not natural or free flowing to be thinking over the ball. A proper release is not body but hands; it's not thinking but fine-tuning and automatic. A new mindset is therefore, a hit mindset.

When you're over the ball, you just think "hit". The old mindset of standing over the ball thinking swing thoughts is just plain wrong. The hit changes your thinking. This is proper mindset.

The Release—Mind at Rest

Let's look at other sports for their mindset. *When you shoot a basketball, what do you think about?* Or *when throwing a football, what do you think about?* Nothing, the mind is at rest. Whether it's shooting pool, throwing darts, or bowling, it all comes down to using hand-eye coordination. I assure you, these athletes are not thinking about technique, their mind is **free** of detailed thinking and has entered into a state of rest. You too can free your mind of swing thoughts by learning a hit.

The Clubface Drill

Practice the hit #1 & #4 by doing our *clubface drill.* Take and 8 iron and place the ball in the middle of your stance. Feet either together or shoulder-width apart. Wrists only take the club to position #1 and hit to position #4. This is what are students practice the first lesson.

The Clubface Drill

The Hit!

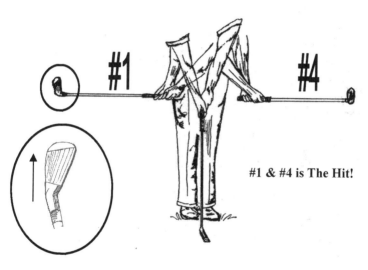

#1 & #4 is The Hit!

When hitting to position #4, use both hands. However, the bottom hand should be used more if this is your dominant hand. Ben Hogan said, *"When releasing the club, I wished that I had three right hands."*

Fine-tuning

When practicing the clubface drill, try not to kill the ball. Remember you are **fine-tuning** the hands on #1 & #4. Your goal is to learn the hit. That's it. Learn it, fine-tune it and hit it!

Sometimes I have a student forget they are fine-tuning and decide they are going to swing the arms and try to kill the ball. Ah, no. I may have to remind them that the objective is to fine-tune the hit, and get the hands coordinated on #1 & #4. In order to get a student fine-tuning again, I will often tell them <u>not</u> to hit the ball out of their shadow. Meaning 20 to 30 yards is all right. Be patient as you learn the hit. This, of course, is a whole new mindset.

Learn it, **Fine-tune it** & Hit it!

Patience

As you fine-tune, understand that you will have a variety of shots that I call: the good, the bad and the ugly. You will top and even miss the ball altogether. These shots are not to be analyzed during the first stages of fine-tuning. This is part of the process and you need to be patient.

When was the last time you awakened your hand-eye coordination? Most likely it was as a child. You tapped into hand-eye coordination daily: to learn tying shoes, throwing or shooting a ball, riding a bike and more. The first time you learned a new task, it was so-so. You got better as you fine-tuned and practiced. As adults, we need to once again tap into hand-eye coordination and fine-tune a new task, which for some may have been a long time ago. You have to have a child's mindset that is willing to learn and keep trying.

At the beginning stage of fine-tuning the hit my students often look at me after bad shots for answers, like I am supposed to say something profound. I remind them they are *fine-tuning*. It's not what a student wants to hear the first 20 to 40 shots, but it's exactly what they need to hear. Be patient when you first learn the hit, it takes time to fine-tune.

What Are Your Goals?

As you learn the hit and continue to fine-tune, have reachable goals. Let's say before lessons you could hit 2 out of 10 shots that you liked. During lessons you progress to hitting 5 out of 10 shots you like. *Are you going to be mad about the 5 you missed? Do you really think you can hit 10 for 10 or 50 for 50 shots?*

The five you missed will get better or maybe not. Sorry, but your hand-eye coordination might not be at the level of a tour pro. Take me for example. Let's face it, I am not 25 anymore. I am older, have three kids, a business and many other day to day responsibilities that limit me from developing hand-eye coordination to what I would like it to be.

Given my circumstances, I may have to be content hitting 8 out of 10 shots that I like. The other two shots should not bother me, because I know my limits. I also know that golf requires other skills, like putting and a shortgame. So when a miss-hit occurs, I can recover with a good chip or putt.

Moving the Hit Higher—Baby Steps

Your next goal is to learn a half of a hit. Only after a student shows consistent fine-tuning on positions #1 & #4, do I have them progress higher to a rib to rib hit, or what I call a *half-hit*. From position #1, simply cup or bend the wrist of your top hand higher to a thumbs up position; what I call 1 1/2. You are now at your ribs. From here, hit to your other rib or 4 1/2. You have just completed a successful half-hit. Fine-tune from rib to rib for awhile. If you start having trouble, go back to the original #1 & #4 positions at waist height.

When practicing a half of a hit, you will notice your arms move and position #4 will be faster. The momentum will cause the body to finish looking like a golf swing. From the original #1 & #4 there is no momentum so it only looks like a hit. Do not be surprised when the hit now looks like a golf swing. Just do not forget that the swing is the effect; just let it happen.

When you are ready, proceed to the next chapter where we will take the hit even higher.

The Upswing at the Top

The upswing is a continuation of the top hand cupping up from the takeaway, meaning keep bending the wrist of the top hand until the wrist stops. This is position #2. Again, two moves are occurring; hands go up, while the shoulders turn slightly. Just do not think about your shoulders. Position #2 is now complete.

Cupping

The Arms

Do not get to #2 by lifting the arms up. It is wrists only that get you to #2. Remember, the arms should follow the hands. When the hands stop, so do the arms. If the arms take over, you will tap into gross-motor skills and leave the fine-tuning stage of the learning process where frustration begins.

The Cupped Hand

Fred Couples says, "I prefer the slightly cupped position which indicates a slightly open clubface, because I know that on the downswing I can really let my wrists whip into the ball with no fear of hitting a wild hook."

The position of the top hand at the top of the swing may also be determined by what grip you use. Some advanced players who have a fast tempo will use a very weak grip. Therefore the top hand will be more flat at the top of position #2. However, the preferred method of *The Ultimate Way* is a stronger grip with a cupped wrist at the top of the swing.

What Golf Swing? It's a Hit: 1,2,3 & 4

The Downswing

From position #2, there needs to be a change of direction to get to the downswing. This direction change is called position #3. The top hand pulls the butt end of the club down about 1 to 2 inches while at the same time keeping your hand cupped. This move is similar to a baseball player hitting a baseball. At the top of the baseball player's backswing, there is a change of direction of the bat, it's only about 1 or 2 inches when the bat is pulled down into position before a batter swings. That change of direction is what I am talking about. Again, it is not noticeable, I do not even see it, but I know if it's missing because you will chunk or hit behind the ball or even come over the top if #3 does not occur. Basically, without #3 there can not be a #4.

So far, if you can execute steps 1, 2 & 3, the club will now be in the hit zone. You should know what to do next; hit the ball at position #4. That's why the clubface drill was practiced so much.

The Hit Zone!

When the downswing or position #3 is complete, you should have your hands just above your ribs by the time your brain understands your hands are now at the ribs. At this time HIT! Turn the clubface to position #4 as fast as you can. With this kind of momentum you will finish showing off what looks like a golf swing to your buddies. Now with proper technique, you can hit as fast as you want; as long as you do not roll the clubface over. Ben Hogan said about the downswing, "Think of only one thing, hitting the ball." If you delay the hit, or hit wrong you will have directional problems; most notably a slice. Or in some instances, a hook results. That is why you practice #1 & #4 between shots.

Hit Zone!

delayed hit = directional problems

Auditory learners should release the clubface with the bottom hand by counting #3 aggressively. A lazy #3 can keep the clubface open; resulting in a slice.

Kinesthetic learners should release the club starting at position (3) and stopping at waist height of the follow-through, called position (4). Refer to the "clubface drill", discussed earlier, to capture this feeling.

The Follow-through or Finish

The follow-through is not something that I teach. Instead of focusing on the follow-through, I focus on stopping at position #4, because momentum will automatically take the club higher. Momentum is based on how fast you can finish #4. *Are your wrists slow or fast?* Your momentum reflects your hand speed. Either way, we all have momentum and this is what makes the hit look like a golf swing. Follow-through, just do not lose focus; your job is to stop at position #4, not your shoulders. Let your momentum do the rest for you.

momentum = a swing

STOP

What Golf Swing? **The Hit—1, 2, 3 & 4!**

Now that you have learned how to hit properly, an automatic golf swing results. This is the principle of cause and effect. Where there is an action, you have a reaction. Learning *The Ultimate Way* ends your search for a perfect golf swing. Just hit 1, 2, 3 & 4. Now you are ready to improve all aspects of your game; from driving, putting, chipping, and more.

It's A Hit!

It's A Hit!

Easy as 1,2,3 & 4!

Taking Lesson to the Course

A question I often get is, *how do I take what I learn from the driving range to the golf course?* Simply stated, *take the clubface drill with you.* This becomes your practice swing.

You probably see other golfers taking full swings on the course. These golfers are not fine-tuning a hit, but rather, they are trying to perfect a golf swing through muscle memory and swing thoughts. This requires too much thinking and ultimately leads to frustration. While these golfers are taking their practice swings, you can fine-tune your hit before each shot by doing the clubface drill #1 & #4. By doing the clubface drill a few times before each shot, perhaps 10 times per hole, or in other words, 180 times per round, you will accomplish a lot of fine-tuning which will make your golf swing automatic in the process.

Using *The Ultimate Way* pre-shot clubface drill routine, is your key to taking what you learn from the range to the golf course.

Course Management

Since the clubface drill eliminates swing thoughts and frees the mind, you can now successfully manage your way around the golf course.

Traditional golfers, who have a swing mindset, will otherwise have a tough time managing the course because they are trying to manage too many swing thoughts at the same time. *Why do you think many tour pros fall apart during a Major?* They are over-thinking. Take swing thoughts about the swing plane or a shoulder turn, and add to that thoughts about a six inch rough, out of bounds on the right, and a 20mph side wind. This is an example of mind overload which, as we have discussed, leads to sheer stress and frustration.

Again, playing golf like this will even get the best of tour pros. Free your mind by eliminating learning a complex golf swing, and you too can manage the golf course.

Properly Fitted Clubs—Did You Know?

Golf is not just about having a proper hitting technique. You should also be aware of lie angles, the driver and other club fitting issues.

Lie Angles

First, a lie angle is how the clubface is bent when hitting the ball. Notice, I said when *hitting*. Some players want their clubs bent because the clubs look too upright or flat at the start. It does not matter what the club looks like at the start. What matters, is what the club looks like when you put the club into action and hit. If the lie angles are in fact incorrect, the hit will also be influenced incorrectly. This too can create a level of frustration that you certainly don't need.

Checking lie angles is easy. All that is needed is a piece of tape stuck on the bottom of each club. Then hit one shot off of a lie board; allowing a mark to appear on the tape. This mark will either appear close to the toe, the heel, or, idealy, in the middle of the club; which means that the lie angle is correct. If the mark is not in the middle, the club needs to be bent correctly.

Too flat   *Too upright*   *Perfect angle*

Measuring a Lie Angle

A proper lie angle must also be measured correctly. A static measurement, where there is no swing, is not accurate.

By placing tape on the bottom of the club and hitting on a lie board, you will be able to tell what the lie angle should be. The majority of golfers should be playing with clubs anywhere from 2 to 5 degrees upright.

Too Flat

It is common for many golfers to have too flat of clubs. This means that the scoring lines of the club are pointing toward the ground at impact. As a result, the ball is hit out toward the toe instead of in the center of the clubface. With the club tilted flat at impact, slice-spin is imparted on the ball. It doesn't matter if the clubface is perfectly square; slice-spin can not be avoided. Playing with flat clubs that create slice-spin, will cause numerous improper changes to the hit. Often these changes occur without even knowing it. The body and clubhead are usually aimed in the opposite direction of the target to compensate for hitting a slice. An outside-in swing results; causing you to cut across the ball. In an attempt to hook the ball, the grip is often made stronger. This change actually closes the clubface which causes the clubface to be opened up even more at impact. If the club is released when closed, a hook results.

Again, too flat of lie angles influences the hit by causing the swing to make improper changes. To improve your hit, you may need to make some minor adjustments to your clubs' lie angles. Consult a respected club fitting professional for assistance.

The scoring lines of the club are pointing toward the ground at impact.

Too Flat

Too Upright

Having a club too upright is not as common. The scoring lines of the club would be pointing up in the air at impact. Thus, the ball will be hit toward the heel. With the club tilted upright at impact, hook-spin will still be imparted on the ball. It doesn't matter if the clubface is perfectly square; hook-spin cannot be avoided.

Playing with upright clubs that create hook-spin will cause numerous improper changes to be made to the hit. Most commonly, reaching for the ball. This causes the weight to be improperly positioned on the feet and the posture to be incorrect. Since hook-spin is imparted on the ball, the tendency is to aim the body and clubface in the opposite direction.

For many, the grip is wrongly blamed for most inconsistencies. So, the grip is often weakened in an attempt to open the clubface. Notice that the short irons are usually hit somewhat far, but pulled. During the swing, an effort will be made to swing inside-out in an attempt to start the ball out to the right *(for right-handed players)*.

Too Upright

56

The club is often not released; causing a push to be hit. Releasing the clubhead from an inside-out swing will cause you to come over-the-top; often hitting a pull or hook shot.

Shorter irons, being more upright than the longer irons, are often blocked open at impact for fear of a hook; causing a slice and loss of distance. Longer irons are hit fairly long, but pulled.

To fix upright clubs, a simple adjustment can be made to bend the club flatter.

Proper Lie Angles

If the lie angles are correct at impact, the soaring lines would be perfectly horizontal; imparting no side-spin on the ball.

Proper Lie Angles

Consider getting your lie angles checked. Changing lie angles is an easy and an affordable adjustment that can be made to a new or older set of clubs. Have your clubs checked by a Professional Clubfitter today.

Standard Clubs May Be Too Short

I discovered early in my teaching career that standard clubs were too short for most players' height. Because of this, my students were blading, topping, losing distance and hitting thin. No matter what I taught, these shots could not be corrected until I made their clubs longer. In some cases this meant a new set of longer clubs all together.

Did you know?
Standard Clubs
Fit a male who is 5'7" to 5'9"
Fit a female who is 5'2" to 5'4"
(Standard weight and no back problems)

Data based on my experiences

Traditional Way to Measure

Retail golf stores traditionally fit clubs to length with a ruler method. The golfer stands straight, arms down with a measurement taken from fingertips to the floor. In my opinion, all the ruler method is designed to do, is sell inventory. Golfers are fit into standard clubs that are on hand. Unfortunately your brand new custom set is still the wrong length, because the ruler method is just not accurate.

Proper Fitting

Fitting someone standing up straight and measuring from the fingertips to the ground, does not give consideration to a person's physical attributes, such as age, ability and weight. I determine length while the golfer is holding the club in the proper setup, while taking into consideration these other aspects.

Age & Ability

Some golfers over the age of 50 should be playing with graphite shafts. They are lighter, easier to swing and take vibration out of the shoulders. A ruler cannot tell you this. Player ability is also a factor. Golfers who swing fast may need special shafts and a head designed specific to their swing speed. Again, a ruler cannot tell you this. Tour pros, for example, have their clubs custom-made from the respected tour departments in which they represent. They do not play standard clubs.

Weight

Today many golfers have issues with being overweight. So even though a golfer may be standard height, their weight determines the need for longer clubs. Furthermore, back issues also determine the need for longer clubs. For example, even though I am standard height, I require longer clubs due to a bad back.

The 50/50 Rule—Did you know?

Improving someone's golf game is a 50/50 combination of custom clubs and golf instruction. You cannot simply focus on one area without focusing on the other.

50% **Proper Instruction**

50% **Properly Fitted Clubs**

Instruction & Proper Clubs = 100%

Both custom clubs and proper golf instruction are essential to improving 100% of your golf game. Great instruction will do nothing if the club is too short. And having the perfect club, will do nothing if you do not know how to hit the ball.

Correcting Miss-Hit Shots

If you are a golfer, you have directional issues. With *The Ultimate Way* you learn how to fix the clubface and not the swing. The ball flight tells you what you are doing wrong. Just fix the clubface and you can avoid all the frustrating swing changes that most golfers try to make and fail.

Slicing —The Solution

Besides the clubs' lie angle possibly being too flat, a slice is hit when the clubface is open at impact. It is a hit problem; not a swing problem. You have to fix the cause; not the effect.

Correct by checking position #1. This is the takeaway where the clubface must be **toe-up**. Now, release the club to position #4, or toe-up at waist height of the forward swing. This allows the clubface to rotate at impact, which causes the ball to go straight and far. The divot will point left, for right-handed golfers, when the ball is hit correctly.

If you are learning how to correct a slice by making swing changes, you will get it all wrong. Trying to fix the effect, such as the grip, alignment, shoulder adjustment, turning the clubface in, and swinging inside out, will be frustrating because you did not fix the cause; the hit. Fix the hit, and you will correct a slice.

Slicing—The Driver

A slice is a slice. The driver is no different. However, it is an aggressive club, so you have to release the club just a little quicker. If you still slice, you have the wrong driver. For instance, you may be playing with the wrong loft, wrong shaft, or too big of head. These issues are addressed in the next chapter.

Auditory learners must first check to see that the clubface is properly opened on the backswing on #1 and #2. When hitting, release the club by counting #3 aggressively. A lazy #3 can keep the clubface open, causing a slice.

Kinesthetic learners need to check the clubface at position #1. When the clubface is correct, be more aggressive releasing the clubface back to a toe-up position at #4 with the bottom hand.

Hooking—The Solution

A ball can only hook if there is counter-clockwise spin or hook-spin imparted on the ball. There are two ways this spin may be applied to the ball. Having a lie angle which is too upright, or hitting with a closed clubface.

Lie angles should be checked by a professional. The clubface should be checked next to see if the takeaway is toe-up at position #1. When hooking, a common mistake is to take the club inside on the takeaway; position #1. When you roll the takeaway on position #1, you will do the same when hitting the ball on position #4.

Fine-tune both positions #1 & #4. On position #1, the shaft must be parallel to the feet with the clubface toe-up. Now you can release the clubface correctly back to a toe-up position at #4. Whereas a hook would be rolling position #4 over with the toe turned sideways. Again, fix position #1 before you fix position #4, because they are a mirror image of each other. The hit is now correct.

Thin Shots

Besides the possibility that your clubs are too short, a thin shot can also occur because you are trying to hit up on the ball at impact. Trying to pick the ball off the ground is simply incorrect mindset. To stop picking the ball, you have to actually get a new visual image of impact. The mistake is that your mental image of impact does not match your technique. Instead of hitting up on the ball, you have to hit down on the ball. The new image of impact is the club striking the top of the ball and rotating down; taking a divot after the ball (*see diagram*). Hitting the ball with proper technique on positions #1& #4 will cause you to hit down properly. You need the image of the club rotating down into the ball and taking a divot after impact. Pros, for example, do not hit up on the ball at impact, but rather, they hit down on the ball. It's like skipping a rock off of water. You have to throw the rock down, for it to skip up. Most golfers do not understand this and try to pick the ball; or hit up, causing it to be hit thin. Both technique and a proper mental image are critical in correcting thin shots.

Look here when hitting.

Do not pick
or hit up.

The clubface rotates down into
the ball at impact, striking
the top, back of the ball.

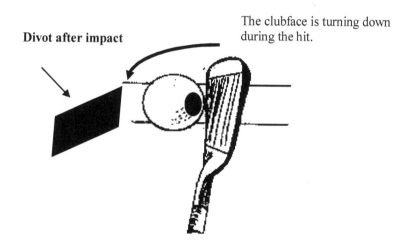

Divot after impact

The clubface is turning down
during the hit.

The Driver

The ball position is off the front heel. The hands point at the front hip; making a straight line with the ball, club, and arm. Notice that more weight is positioned on the back foot during the set-up. This encourages you to hit up on the ball at impact which is acceptable with longer clubs that are played more forward in your stance. You will also feel like your head is behind the ball during the set-up. Now you are ready to hit.

Wrong Loft

Many golfers are trying to play with an 8 to 10 degree driver when they should not. This loft is for golfers who can hit the ball over 250 yards. Since many golfers do not hit that far, a higher lofted driver would match the swing speed better; producing more distance and better direction. I would recommend a driver of 10.5 to 14 degrees if you hit the ball 250 yards or less.

With a higher loft, you get better direction. That is why I never have anyone complain that they slice their 48 degree wedge, or even their 15 degree 3 wood. Go up in loft if you want better direction.

This does not mean you won't slice. You still have to have proper technique in hitting the ball, so work on positions #1 & #4 with an eight iron. Yes, an iron makes the driver work better. If you can't hit an iron, you can't hit a driver.

The Driver Loft & Distance

The truth is, most golfers are hitting the wrong loft on a driver and losing a lot of distance. Using a 6 degree driver will result in about 2000 rpm of spin, while using a 14 degree driver with the same speeds will result in about 3000 rpm of spin.

Take the same swing and change only the loft to 14 degrees, and the ball will have more spin or rpms. The result is greater distance and better accuracy.

Information obtained from UG&A Teaching advisor A.J. Bonar (Taylor Made Studies)

- A 6 degree driver will hit the ball 155 yards.
- A 14 degree club will hit the ball 200 yards.

Do you hit your 3 wood further than your driver? Consider changing to a more lofted driver if you do.

The Ultimate Way **Preferred Lofts**
(based on distance you can hit)

14 degree driver = 150—190 yards
12 degree driver = 190—210 yards
11 degree driver = 210—230 yards
10 degree driver = 230—280 yards
9 degree driver = 280—320 yards

Slicing: The Shaft

A shaft that is too flexible can cause the clubface to stay open; resulting in a slice. You may need a shaft that allows you to swing faster. I often hear people who have fast swings say, "I would like to swing fast, but I do better when I slow my swing down". I say hogwash! You just need the right shaft and then learn to swing for the fence!

If you hit over 300 yards, you may need to ditch your stiff-flex for an (x) or (xx) shaft. I have one student who swings so fast that he has a (xxxxx) shaft. He can hit over 413 yards in long drive competitions where the fairway is only 40 yards wide. With his old shaft, he could only hit about 320 yards.

Driving can be very rewarding if you have the correct club in your bag. Get fitted properly for shaft flex and you can eliminate the shaft from causing a slice while driving.

Size of the Driver Head

Do you realize that bigger driver heads don't mean better performance? You can hit the ball better with a smaller driver head. A larger driver head of 410 cc to 460 cc can actually make releasing the club harder, causing a slice. Try hitting a smaller head with proper technique and you may find it easier to keep the ball from slicing.

Putting Fundamentals

P utting is more of an art than anything else. The focus should be to develop a consistent putting stroke that controls distance and helps you avoid a three putt. The key to a consistent putting stroke is to use only the dominant hand and shoulders. Too often the ball is blasted past the hole. This is an indication that you are trying to use both hands, which creates confusion. When putting, eliminate confusion by using only your dominant hand. The other hand is just on the club for looks.

One-Handed Practice Drill:
First practice putting one-handed with only the dominant hand. Once you feel more consistent, place the other hand back on the club. Your other hand should do nothing except guide. This drill is very effective.

Putting—Judging Distance
Judging distance seems to be one of the most common mistakes when putting. Many golfers just use the wrong technique. Simply trying to hit harder or softer is an inconsistent method. To hit the ball the correct distance, your backswing should match your follow-through. If you want to hit the ball a shorter distance, shorten your backswing and match the follow-through. Having the same backswing and follow-through are key to consistent putting. To practice this technique I have come up with a simple drill.

Ten Foot Putt Drill
Pick a normal ten foot putt and practice taking the putter back 5 inches on the backswing and the same on the follow-through. See how far the ball travels. Adjust the backswing and follow-through 1inch for every three feet the ball is long or short.

Once you figure the distance for a ten foot putt, practice a thirteen foot putt by adding 1 inch to the backswing and forward swing. Keep adding 1 inch for every three feet you add. The common method of hitting harder or softer is no longer the method of choice. Try *The Ultimate Way*.

Ten Foot Putt

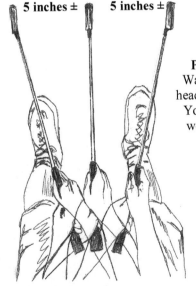

5 inches ±   5 inches ±

Putting Tip:
Watch the putter head when putting. You can avoid a wobbly putting stroke.

It works!

Example:

Ten foot putt = about 5 inches ±
Thirteen foot putt = about 6 inches ±
Sixteen foot putt = about 7 inches ±
(And so forth.)

± *subject to change, based on personal tempo and greens*

Note: *About 3 feet is gained on your putt for every inch added to the backswing and follow-through. This is subject to change with fast or slow greens, up-hill or down-hill putts.*

The Grip

When putting, the grip is strictly a personal preference. If you are a beginner, use the same grip as with your irons and woods. More advanced players can experiment with a variety of different grip styles.

In any case, the grip must avoid tension. I have found this is best achieved with larger putter grips. Now I am referring to the actual grip on the club. A standard size putter grip is too small, as it allows the putter to move around in the hands. When this occurs, the putter head is also twisting and keeps the club head from staying square.

Therefore, the grip I often recommend is three times larger than a regular size putter grip. Try it. It really works.

Ball Position When Putting

When putting, play the ball in the middle of the stance or off the front heel; strictly a personal preference.

Reading Greens—A Lost Art

Reading greens is not technique; however, it is your most important part of putting. Read, aim and hit, or **R.A.H**, is a system of putting that decreases awareness by shifting the focus away from mechanics. Instead, it stresses the most important aspect of becoming a great putter, which is reading greens. By focusing on the mechanics, as many do, frustration is created. Comments like, *"I pushed it"* or *"I pulled it"*, say that there is too much focus on mechanics.

The R.A.H system breaks down putting into the following by importance. First, **read** the green. You must do this before you can hit the putt. Reading a green is 80% of importance. Many golfers do not take time to read the green or know how. If reading a green is avoided, one will not be a good putter. Once the green is read, **aim** the putter-head to the target. Aiming the putter-head to the intended line is 12% of importance. Once the putt is read and aimed, just **hit** the ball. Hitting the ball, or mechanics, is 8% of importance. *What do you focus on?*

The Yips

When a player has the yips, thinking about direction, instead of speed, will get them back to putting with confidence.

Most golfers just aim at the hole; not knowing how to read a green. This causes many easy putts to be missed.

Reading Greens: What to Look for

Reading greens is judging how the grain and slope affect the ball's direction and speed. Gathering information on grain and slope will tell you where to aim the putt. If the putt is *read* wrong, you will not make the putt; regardless of how well you aimed and hit the ball.

Grain

Once you have considered the slope, take into consideration the grain. Depending upon the direction in which the grain is growing, it will increase or decrease the slope's influence. If the grain is growing in the same direction as the slope, the putt will be extra *fast,* and it will break more. If the grain is growing in the opposite direction of the slope, the putt will be *slower,* and not break as much.

Tip: Identifying the Grain

If the grain or grass looks dull, the putt will be slow. If the grain looks shiny, then the putt will be fast. The ability to test the grain can only be done by sight. The Rules of Golf do not permit touching the green to test the surface. This would be a penalty in tournaments. However, you can walk over to the apron where the grass is longer and touch it. This will give you a better idea as to what direction the grass may be growing on the green. Focus your attention on reading the green and not so much on technique. You too can become a great putter.

Slope

Stand or slightly squat behind the ball to see the slope. Slope is determined by the contour of the green. Whether the putt is up-hill, down-hill, left to right or right to left, take the slope into consideration when determining speed and where to aim.

Putting Routine

When putting, I use the following routine. First, I check the grain of the grass in front of the ball to see what direction it is growing. Next, I walk to the cup to look at the grain there. The grain will either point left, right, straight to the ball, or straight going away from the ball. All this will affect the direction and speed of the ball when putting. From the cup, I then determine the length of the putt as I walk back to the ball. Now, back behind the ball, I look at the slope. I will check to see if the putt breaks left or right, down-hill or up-hill. Now taking all into consideration, let me walk you through my putting routine from start to finish.

My ball is 10 feet from the hole. The first thing I do is check out the grain. I walk to the hole to determine the direction. The grain is moving left. I conclude that the ball will move about a 1/2 inch left due to grain only. I walk 5 feet behind the ball looking back to determine slope. I determine the slope breaks

left 3 inches. When I add a grain of a 1/2 inch left, I have a putt that breaks 3 1/2 inches left. The slope also helps me determine speed. Since this putt breaks, I will change my 5 inch putt to 4 1/2 inches. I walk up to the ball and take a 4 1/2 inch practice putt, and then I hit the ball in the hole.

Many recreational golfers may choose not to follow such a specific routine. However, when you are playing for score, or if golf is your profession, then having some kind of system for reading greens. A putting routine is mathematical and a true art at the same time. Once you learn what to look for, you too can make more putts than ever before!

Shortgame Fundamentals

When chipping close to the green, hit a shot called a chip & run. A low shot that runs like a putt. The club is taken back like a putter; a shoulder-arm swing with no wrist-cock. Most importantly, your weight should remain on your front foot.

Chip & Run Setup:

> **Important:** 90% of your weight is on the front foot. Keep your hands ahead of the club after impact.

Technique
- Position the hands slightly ahead of the ball.
- Position most of your weight on your front foot.
- The ball position should be in the middle of your stance.

Chip & Run—Distance Control

Distance control, when chipping, seems to be a mystery to many. Practice using one club; a sand wedge. Try to hit this club using the same length backswing and follow-through. This will develop a consistent tempo. When the tempo and length are the same, you will start to hit several shots the same distance. Maybe 20 feet. This is good.

Let's say you want to hit about 30 feet. Now instead of changing tempo, change clubs. Choose a 9 iron. The loft of the club will allow you to hit about 3 to 5 feet further. The secret to chipping consistently is to change your club selection, not your tempo.

The following is my club selection based on my tempo on a flat green with normal green speed.

15 feet = Lob Wedge
20 feet = Sand Wedge
25 feet = Pitching Wedge
30 feet = 9 Iron
35 feet = 8 Iron
40 feet = 7 Iron
45 feet = 6 Iron
50 feet = 5 Iron

Chipping—Reading the Green

Read the green before choosing the best club. You may have to use a more lofted or less lofted club depending upon whether the chip is uphill or downhill. Next recognize the speed of the green, as you may have to adjust to faster or slower greens. Other factors influence club selection as well. Consider if you are you chipping into or with the wind.

At times you will have more than one factor to consider when chipping. You may have a fast green that is downhill with wind at your back. For example, a 9 iron chip may now need to be a lob wedge chip. Taking into consideration your surroundings is the art of reading greens. It takes some experience to become a great chipper. Technique can be taught, however; reading the green must be experienced. A chipper who is used to the surroundings and easily reads what is around them, will be the best chipper.

Shortgame—-Hitting Fat or Thin

Simply adjust your set-up to stop hitting fat or thin when hitting a short shot around the green. Mistakes occur because you shift your weight to your back foot. A fat shot will occur first; and then you'll rise up and start hitting it thin. No one likes to chunk the ball by the green or send it thin across the green. A simple adjustment, keeping the weight on your front foot throughout the hit, will prevent you from hitting fat or thin.

When chipping, place approximately 80-90% of your weight on the front foot during the hit.

When pitching, place approximately 70-80% of your weight on the front foot during the hit.

Pitching—The Setup

What is a pitch shot? A shot that is usually hit over 30 yards. Unlike chipping, this shot involves the use of wrists; just like hitting a normal golf shot. The set-up is the same as when chipping. Use an open stance and put about 70 to 80% weight on the front foot.

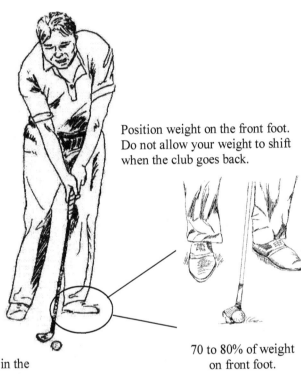

Position weight on the front foot. Do not allow your weight to shift when the club goes back.

Play the ball in the middle of your stance.

70 to 80% of weight on front foot.

Auditory learners need to count #1 and then #2 for the hit. Counting creates rhythm when pitching.

Kinesthetic learners need to feel. Start by hitting waist height to waist height shots. This will create a feel. Next add 6 inches, hitting to the ribs: Finally hit to the breast bone. Stop at each position to get a feel and make sure you stop at the equal position on the follow-through to check distance control.

Pitching Distance Control: Sand Wedge (SW)

Set-up with an open stance, putting 70 to 80% weight on the front foot. For distance control when pitching, simply stop the hands at the same length on the backswing as on the follow-through. First stop at position 1 & 4. Lets say you hit a 30 yard shot. Now to hit a 40 yard shot, proceed with the same set-up, but take your wrists 6 inches higher to position 1.5. The thumbs should be pointing straight up. Hit the ball stopping at the same equal spot on the follow-through; in other words 4.5. To hit a 50 yard shot, slightly bend the thumbs back at position 1.75 and finish at 4.75. Again, the thumbs should be pointing slightly back at your chest. Using this method controls distance and creates consistency. You can do the same technique with a lob wedge (lw), giving you more distance choices *(see note below)*.

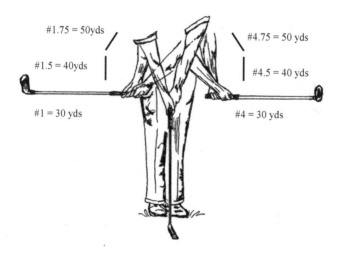

#1.75 = 50yds
#1.5 = 40yds
#1 = 30 yds

#4.75 = 50 yds
#4.5 = 40 yds
#4 = 30 yds

Add Lob Wedge: I use this same distance control with my lob wedge, giving me more distance choices than hitting with just a sand wedge. For instance: when I hit 1 & 4 with my lob wedge, this gives me about 25 yards, hitting 1.5 to 4.5, about 35 yards and hitting 1.75 to 4.75, about 45 yards.

Bunker Shots

Set more square to the target while hitting a bunker shot. When in a fairway bunker, consider your club selection carefully. Pick the club that gets you over the lip of the bunker, not necessarily on the green. Remain still when hitting.

Green Side Bunker

With a green side bunker shot, look about 1 inch behind the ball rather than at the back of the ball. Hitting behind the ball allows the sand to send the ball onto the green. Keep the lower body still and let the length of the swing determine the distance.

Tee drill: to hit 1 inch behind the ball, place a tee under the ball and visualize breaking the tee in half.

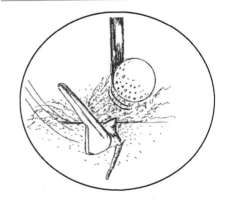

Buried Lie—In Bunker

For a buried lie, swing the club back more V-shaped and then chop down into the sand. The explosion will throw the ball out of the sand. This technique may also be used when hitting out of deep grass.

Use a "V"-shaped swing in the bunker.

Specialty Shots

O n a windy day, try to hit the ball low to increase control and accuracy. With a driver, set the tee lower and follow-through lower after impact. For irons, place the ball slightly back in the stance to allow the hands to be ahead of the ball. Set-up to the ball with about 60% of your weight on the front foot. Shorten your back-swing and follow-through to a half hit. Your club selection will change too. Normally where I would hit a 9 iron, I would select a 7 iron. *Why?* My swing is shorter to help keep the ball down, so now I need more club to make up for a shorter swing. You too, will need to adjust club selection based on your ability and the conditions around you.

Awkward Lies
Having the ball in the middle of the fairway is everyone's goal. However, depending on your lie, this may be challenging. The following describes how right-handers should set-up for awkward lies.

Uphill Lie
- Shoulders should follow the incline of the terrain.
- Use a less-lofted club.
- Choke down on the club.
- Aim right of the target; the ball will have a tendency to go left.

Downhill Lie
- Use a club with additional loft.
- Play the ball back in your stance.
- Hit downward with the slope.
- Aim left of the target: the ball will have a tendency to go right.

Sidehill Lie, Ball Above Feet

- Position your weight on your toes to prevent falling backward.
- Choke down on the club.
- Aim right of the target: the ball will have a tendency to go left.

Sidehill Lie, Ball Below Feet

- Position your weight on your heels to prevent falling forward.
- Choke up on the club.
- Aim left of the target: the ball will have a tendency to go right.

Ultimate Practice Routine

The ultimate practice routine allows you to take what you learn from the range to the course. The secret is to take #1 & #4 with you as your new practice swing before each shot. While others are taking practice swings, my students are taught to fine-tune the hit with the clubface drill before each shot. Sure, this will get others to notice and ask questions, but let them. You will find the ultimate practice routine works if you follow it from start to finish.

Start: On the Range

Begin your practice session on the range by hitting 30, 40, & 50 yard shots with a sand wedge or a lob wedge. These short shots fine-tune the hit and improve your shortgame at the same time, which in fact, may be the most important shot for anyone who wants to improve their golf game.

Proceed

Continue from hitting pitch shots to every other club. Hit 5 to 10 balls with each club. If one club is causing problems, stay with that club until confidence is built, then move to another club. So hit your PW, 8, 6, 4, fairway wood, and finally your driver. Then alternate your odd clubs another day.

Finish

Finish your practice session the same as you started; hitting 30 yard pitch shots. This helps you end with more confidence and make final adjustments to your hitting technique if need be.

Putting Green

First, find a ten foot putt and hit several putts to determine distance of back and through. Some golf courses are fast, so a 10 foot putt may only require 5 inches back and through, while other greens require 6 inches back and through. Keep adding inches for longer putts, making sure your backswing and forward swing match. Finally, end your putting practice with several shorter putts to gain confidence.

Chip Shots

Next, hit a few chips close to the green. Again, start by determining how far you hit your sand wedge. All your other clubs are based off of this club. For example, my sand wedge goes about 20 feet on normal greens, so I know I gain about 3 to 5 feet for each club. If I have a 25 foot chip, I then use a PW. If I have a 30 foot chip, I then use a 9 iron and so on.

Pitch Shots

Since you have already hit pitch shots on the driving range, you are ready to proceed to the golf course.

On the Course

How do you take what you learn on the range with you to the golf course? Again, take the clubface drill with you. This is what you should practice before each shot. When others are taking golf swings in their attempt to manage swing thoughts, I want you practicing the hit; fine-tuning and not thinking. Follow these steps.

1. Do (2) clubface drills before each shot.
2. Set up to the ball.
3. Hit it!

If you continue with this routine several times before each shot, you will have fine-tuned over 150 times per round; getting more automatic all the time. You will have successfully taken what you learned on the range with you to the golf course.

For the Good of the Game

S low play is a major problem all golf courses are faced with today. In fact, many golf courses have "rangers" or other means to monitor slow play. The following are suggestions to help you speed up play and still enjoy your time on the golf course.

The Beverage Cart
- Do not stop the beverage cart in the middle of the fairway or by the green. Be aware that the group behind wants to hit. The beverage cart driver has no idea they can slow up play, but often do when stopping in the wrong spot. Do them a favor, and wave them to the next tee.

The Tee Box
- Have your equipment ready: tees, proper club, and more than one golf ball for errant shots. Limit mulligans on the first tee, especially if the course is busy.
- Play the proper set of tees based on your ability. You will more enjoyment from a shorter set of tees.
- Play ready-golf on every shot, especially if you're behind.
- Try not to stand and watch your playing partner go through his/her routine without getting ready yourself.

The Fairway
- While a player is hitting, the rest of the group should be choosing a club and calculating yardage.
- Limit the number of practice swings, especially if you have been warned by a ranger to pick up the pace.
- Keep pace with the group <u>ahead</u>. Do not be concerned with the group behind: even if you cannot see them.
- If weather conditions prevent driving carts in the fairway, take more than one club out to your ball.

The Green
- Park the golf cart between the green and the next tee box.
- Place your golf bag on the exit side of the green by the next tee.
- Prepare to putt while someone else is putting.
- Finish gimme putts.
- Prepare to putt out of turn if someone is not ready.
- Mark scores at the next tee box, not on the green.

Etiquette: Tee to Green
When starting out for the first time, you should learn proper etiquette; the do's and don'ts on the course. For example, where to stand when teeing off. It can be nerve-racking just trying to make it through a round without losing a dozen golf balls. The following are tips to assist you when you go out to play your next round of golf...

Tee Box & Fairway
- Honors; whoever had the best score after the first hole, would tee off first on the next hole. The person with the second best score would follow and so on. That person would only lose honors if someone should get a better score on another hole.
- Do not make any noise during someone's swing.
- If pace of play is an issue, play "ready golf". That means whoever is on the tee first, hits first. However, still try to give honors to a birdie from the previous hole no matter how fast you are trying to play.

The Green
- The player furthest from the hole putts first.
- The player closest to the hole tends the pin only if someone cannot see the hole.
- If you are tending the pin ask, "can everyone see the hole?" If someone cannot see the hole, stand by the hole and pull the pin out as the ball moves closer to the hole. Then lay the

pin off to the side; far enough away so no one can hit the pin when they putt. If the ball hits the pin, it is a penalty.

The Putting Line
- The putting line, from the player's ball to the hole, is a sacred line. That line is not to be touched by anyone.
- Respect a player's line; do not walk on it or cast a shadow on it.
- If a player is not looking at his or her line, you may straddle over it.
- If a player is looking at his or her line, walk around the player.

NOTE: If you are not sure whether or not your actions are disturbing others, common sense should always prevail.

Terminology
The is a list of the most commonly used terms.

Scoring Terms
- **Par-**The number of shots required to finish the hole.
- **Birdie-**One better or under par.
- **Eagle-**Two better or under par.
- **Double Eagle-**Only on par 5s, in which the ball is hit in on the second shot. (This does not happen very often because a second shot is usually hit too far away.)
- **Hole-in-one-**On a par 3 and sometimes a par 4. The ball is hit in on your first shot. Celebrate! Keep the ball as a reminder and pay the bar bill.
- **Bogie-**One more than par.
- **Double Bogie-**Two more than par.
- **Triple Bogie-**Three more than par.
- **Quadruple Bogie or Snowman-**Four more than par. A par four with four strokes over would be an 8, which is called a *snowman.* Anything more than four over par, control your temper; you probably have your own name for this!

Directional Terms

- **Slice-**The ball curves off to the right for right-handers.
- **Hook-**The ball curves off to the left for right-handers.
- **Hitting Fat-**When the club hits turf behind the ball.
- **Hitting Thin-**When you catch the ball on the upswing and the ball goes low.
- **Shank-**The ball catches off the hosel and usually goes bad to the right. In golf, a shank is a four letter word, even though it is five letters.
- **Topping-**When your club hits the top of the ball, causing it to lift up and fall back to the ground.
- **Blading-**When the club catches the top of the ball and causes it to move low to the ground.

Clubs 101

The tee box: For long holes, hit the driver and tee it up. Some golfers have trouble hitting the driver and should hit a 3 or 5 wood. On shorter holes that are called par 3s, you have to hit a club for the yardage of the hole. This means knowing how far you hit each club, which takes some practice to know. For example, I hit my 7 iron about 175 yards.

The fairway: Golfers who do not hit very far should use a 7 or 5 wood and perhaps a hybrid. As you get closer to the hole, start to use your irons. A 100 yard shot for the average player may be a sand wedge. However, a beginner might use an 8 iron. Knowing your 100 yard clubs takes some practice on the range.

The green: When just off the green, you would be chipping. This can involve several clubs, but the main clubs would be a sand wedge or pitching wedge. When actually on the green, use your putter.

References

Kathlene Bissell, *Fred Couples (2000) pg 31*
Total shotmaking: The golfer's guide to low scoring (1995), pg 31

80% to 20% of brain Page 26
  http://wings.buffalo.edu/aru Chpt08.ppt#293,14, Corticospinal Tract

The Brain Page 25-26
  http://www.stumblerz.com/brain-fun-facts/
  http://library.thinkquest.org/J002391/functions.html
  http://www.ag.ndsu.edu/pubs/yf/famsci/fs609w.htm
  http://www.physpharm.fmd.uwo.ca/undergrad/medsweb/L5Motor/
    Motor.swf

Made in the USA
Charleston, SC
13 July 2011